MOLLY McCLOG

Written by Telene Clarke-Giles
Illustrated by David Kennett

There once was a farmer
named Molly McClog,

Who had a white goat
    and a green bullfrog.
The goat it was hairy;
    the frog it was fat,

But Molly McClog
didn't care about that.

There once was a farmer
named Molly McClog,
Who had a brown cow
and a spotty old dog.

The cow it was wide;
the dog it was fat,
But Molly McClog
didn't care about that.

There once was a farmer
named Molly McClog,
Who had a black hen
and a grunting hog.

The hen it was plump;
the hog it was fat,
But Molly McClog
didn't care about that.

There once was a farmer
named Molly McClog,
Who had a grey possum
that slept in a log.

The log it was large;
the possum was fat,
But Molly McClog
didn't care about that.

There once was a farmer
named Molly McClog,

Who lived with a goat
and a fat bullfrog . . .

A wide brown cow
  and a spotty old dog,
A plump black hen
  and a grunting hog,

And a fat grey possum
that slept in a log.

But Molly found out
when she called them all in,

That the pets were too fat
and the house too thin!

First published by Era Publications,
220 Grange Road, Flinders Park, South Australia 5025

Concept drawings by Carol McLean-Carr
Printed in Hong Kong
First Published 1996

National Library of Australia
Cataloguing-in-Publication Data:
Clarke-Giles, Telene
Molly McClog.

ISBN 1 86374 242 5

1. Readers (Primary). 2. Animals - Juvenile poetry.
3. Children's poetry, Australian. I. Kennett, David, 1959-
II. Title. (Series: Magic bean).

428.6

Available in:

Australia from Era Publications, 220 Grange Road,
Flinders Park, South Australia 5025

Canada from Vanwell Publishing Ltd, 1 Northrup Cresc., PO Box 2131, Stn B,
St Catharines, ONT L2M 6P5

New Zealand from Reed Publishing, 39 Rawene Road,
Birkenhead, Auckland 10

Singapore, Malaysia & Brunei from Publishers Marketing Services
Pty Ltd, 10-C Jalan Ampas, #07-01 Ho Seng Lee Flatted Warehouse, Singapore 1232

United Kingdom from Heinemann Educational Publishers,
Halley Court, Jordan Hill, Oxford OX2 8EJ

United States of America from Australian Press ™,
c/- Ed-Tex, 15235 Brand Blvd, #A107, Mission Hills CA 91345